# AMANDA KLOOTS

# Tell Me Your Dreams

Illustrated by ALEX WILLMORE

HARPER
An Imprint of HarperCollinsPublishers

Tell Me Your Dreams

Text copyright © 2023 by Amanda Kloots

Illustrations copyright © 2023 by Alex Willmore

All rights reserved. Manufactured in Italy.

No part of this book may be used or reproduced in any manner whatsoever
without written permission except in the case of brief quotations embodied in
critical articles and reviews. For information address HarperCollins Children's
Books, a division of HarperCollins Publishers, 195 Broadway, New York, NY 10007.

www.harpercollinschildrens.com

Library of Congress Control Number: 2022947975
ISBN 978-0-06-322511-4

The artist used mixed media, pencil on paper, and
Adobe Photoshop to create the digital illustrations for this book.
Book design by Jeanne Hogle
23  24  25  26  27   RTLO   10  9  8  7  6  5  4  3  2  1


First Edition

It's bedtime.
Cozy pajamas, favorite lovey, warmest blanket.
Special bedtime rocking chair.

Mama will tuck you into bed and you will go sleepy.

Honk shooo,
honk shooo.

And when you're
asleep . . . that's
when you dream.

Do you want me to tell you your dreams?

YES!

In your dreams, anything is possible. In your dreams, you can go anywhere. Do everything. See anyone.

Tonight, in your dreams . . .
Trash truck!

Okay! Tonight, in your dreams, a trash truck appears in your room!

What color is it? Green!

And who's driving that big green trash truck? Dada!

That's right! So, you get into the trash truck and start driving down the street.

All of a sudden, that trash truck turns into a big airplane!

You're flying over the neighborhood and into the clouds.

Whee!

And look!

The clouds are made of

The rainbow sprinkles turn into a real rainbow and you fly your airplane

right through it. Where do you go now? The beach!

You land on the warm sand.

Okay! You build the longest choo-choo ever.

It's glittering in the sun as Dada says, "All aboard!"

You step inside the train with Dada.
This time he lets you drive.

Yeah!

You drive the choo-choo into the ocean, gliding over the water. It goes faster . . . and faster! Chugga-chugga-chugga!

Dolphins swim by. They jump up to give you a high five!

Before you know it, you're back in your room, safe and sound.

Dada tucks you into your bed. He gives you the biggest hug ever. "I love you," he whispers. And what do you say?

I love you, Dada.

In the morning, you can tell me
all about your dream.
   Where you went. What you did.
And who you saw.

But for now, it's time to go sleepy.

Sweet dreams.